This Notebook belongs to:

____

– Independently Published –

Legal Notice:

S_DESIGN
Sebastian Epkes
Chan 43 Yaek 26
Bangkok 10120
Thailand
see_the_lite@gmx.de